D1368303

J.
636.8

BARRON'S

Astrid Schubert

My Cat
and me

Photographs: Monika Wegler
Illustrations: Renate Holzner

Stories: Gabriele Linke-Grün

57496

Contents

Building Trust from the Start

love it

Cat Adventures

Fun and Games with Cats

have fun

Active and Happy in Old Age

old & happy

Golden

As Contessa stalks her prey, every muscle in her elegant body is tuned to one purpose— the hunt. All cats are born hunters and need plenty of opportunities for physical activity, whether outdoors or indoors. If you give your cat proper care, a balanced diet of nutritious food, and lots of petting and attention, you'll have a healthy and happy pet.

Rules
for Proper Care

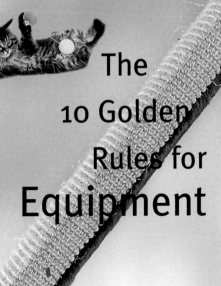

The 10 Golden Rules for Equipment

1 A basket with a soft pillow makes a cozy place for kitty to sleep or just relax.

2 Each cat needs a round food bowl and water dish that won't slip, with a minimum diameter of 6 inches (15 cm).

3 Never place the food bowl and water dish next to the cat's litter box.

4 Basic rule for the number of litter boxes: For single cats, provide a box large enough for the cat to enter, turn around, cover its excrement without stepping in it, and exit. In multi-cat households, provide a litter box for each cat, place them in different rooms, if possible, and clean each twice a week.

5 All cats require a sturdy scratching post to sharpen their claws.

6 An indoor climbing structure serves as a scratching post and offers good exercise as well.

7 A cat feels safe when it can sit in an elevated spot with a view of its surroundings.

8 A plastic cat carrier is useful for trips to the veterinarian, for example.

9 An automatic food dispenser comes in handy if you need to be away for a day or two.

10 A collar with nametag has brought many a lost kitty home. Choose one with a safety buckle or breakaway insert so the cat won't choke if the collar snags.

take care

The 10 Golden Rules for Feeding

1 Cats are carnivores. Their diet should include some meat protein. Premium dry cat foods are formulated with plenty of animal-source meat protein.

2 Dog food is not good for cats as a basic diet, because the quality and source of protein in dry dog food are not the same as those in premium dry cat food.

3 Feed your cat on a regular schedule. Morning and evening is best.

4 Provide a varied diet—commercial cat food in the morning, and some suitable cat snacks at night.

5 Treats are fine, but offer them sparingly, or the cat may become a finicky eater.

6 Cats appreciate a clean feeding area. Wash the food and water bowls with hot water every day.

7 Serve cat food as fresh as possible, and preferably at room temperature.

8 Spicy, salty, or sugary table scraps are hard for cats to digest.

9 A cat must have fresh drinking water available at all times. This is especially important if you feed your kitty dry cat food.

10 Cat grass (or digestive aids from the veterinarian) can help cats to digest their food.

The 10 Golden Rules for Care

1 Depending on the length of your cat's hair, you will need a brush with soft bristles, a rubber brush, or a fine-tooth metal comb.

2 Short-haired cats should be brushed daily only in spring and fall, when they are shedding. It's best to comb a long-haired kitty every day.

3 Long-haired cats can be bathed with a cat shampoo if their coat gets very dirty.

4 Every cat should visit the veterinarian once a year for a physical examination and vaccinations.

5 To prevent fleas in the spring and summer, keep your cat indoors.

6 Check your cat's teeth regularly for tartar buildup.

7 Use a soft, damp cloth to remove crusty deposits in the corner of a cat's eyes.

8 Wipe out your kitty's ears with a paper towel, but don't attempt to clean deep inside them.

9 Once a day, scoop feces and wet litter from every litter box. Replenish with fresh litter.

10 Once a week, empty the litter box and scrub it with hot water, then fill it with fresh litter.

Typical

On their first spring outing, Shadow and Moxie revel in the green grass and fragrant flowers. Kittens grow up very quickly, because cats in the wild are on their own at an early age. Fortunately, Shadow and Moxie don't need to worry—they have a good home.

Cats

How Did Cats Become Domesticated?

Our domestic cats all descend from wild cats that were caught and tamed long ago. Nobody knows for certain how or where cats were first tamed, but cats are now common household pets.

The cat—as ever—had an independent spirit from the start. Unlike other animals, cats came to live with people by their own choice. At first, more and more wild cats made their way to the vicinity of human settlements, where grain was stored and mice and rats were plentiful. Cats that had once lived as more or less solitary creatures now grew accustomed to living in groups, because they no longer had to compete with each other for limited prey. Though farmers regarded the rodents that overran their barns as pests, the cats found them delicious. People soon realized that cats could be very useful in keeping the rodent population under control, and they began to welcome their presence, offer them shelter, and treat them as pets. Over the course of centuries, cats evolved from wild animals into the many breeds of cats we know today.

Unlike other domesticated animals, today's cats—whether Persian or Siamese, purebred or crossbred—still retain all the skills of their wild ancestors, and they can survive without the help of humans. However, most cats welcome contact with people and greatly appreciate the comforts of home.

If a plump fish is the reward, cats will even overcome their natural distaste for getting wet.

Foxy and Moxie

Moxie came into the world on January 1, 2000—a true millennium cat. When I first met him, I knew right away that this spirited little tomcat was something special. But how would he get along with Foxy, our Abyssinian? And what should we name him? Foxy, who was born with a bright rusty-red coat and a cunning look on his mischievous face, had been easy to name, but I pondered all the way home about what to call our newest kitten.

After the long car ride, the little fellow was eager to explore his new home. I chose to introduce him to Foxy in the kitchen. As soon as Foxy set eyes on the newcomer, he arched his back, bristled his fur, and hissed fiercely. He obviously wanted to make it clear from the start who was in charge. But the kitten was not the least bit impressed by Foxy's show of force. With his head held high and his tail erect, he marched proudly past the Abyssinian and leaped onto the counter. From this vantage point, he gazed down at Foxy with an air of friendly curiosity. Foxy, in turn, was visibly annoyed. For want of any better response, he turned away and began to groom himself with great intensity. Chuckling to myself at the kitten's courage, I thought, "What moxie!" From that moment, our new kitten had his name—and I'm happy to report that Foxy and Moxie are now the best of friends.

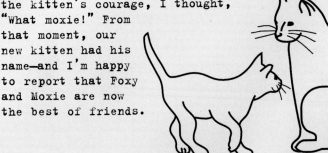

People in cultures around the world admire cats for their agility, beauty, and mystery. The ancient Egyptians considered cats sacred. They worshiped a goddess of love and fertility, Bastet, whom they depicted with the head of a cat and the body of a woman. In Chinese mythology, these charming feline hunters offer protection against evil spirits. In Europe in the Middle Ages, though, superstitious people associated the cat with witchcraft and the Devil; hundreds of thousands of cats were killed. The resulting explosion in the rat population may well have led to the widespread plague known as the Black Death. Fortunately, this sad chapter in history eventually ended, and cats regained their popularity. In the mid-19th century, cat fanciers began to breed cats for particular characteristics, giving rise to the variety of breeds known today. But the long-haired Persian, the supple Oriental, and the hardy barn cat all have their origins in the wild feline that decided, all on its own, to come in from the wild, and ended up—fed and petted—in the warm and cozy living room.

Territoriality

Cats are territorial creatures, although their need for their own

What Cats Are Like

➜ House cats need plenty of entertainment and attention from their owners.

➜ All cats are naturally curious. This means that young cats, in particular, often lead a dangerous life.

➜ Cats love to play. Over time, each kitty develops its own favorite games.

➜ Cats are meat-eaters and require a good amount of animal protein in their diet.

➜ Cats tend to be more active at twilight and in the evening hours.

➜ Cats like to rest on high platforms, where they feel protected.

➜ Cats prefer a peaceful environment. If there's too much hustle and bustle, they will find a quiet retreat.

➜ Cats have excellent hearing. Blaring music or other loud noises bother them.

➜ Cats see very well, even in twilight. This is when mice and other rodents—their natural prey—are most active.

space may vary widely. Many are satisfied to claim a favorite chair; others must have the whole house to themselves and will not tolerate the presence of any other cat. These cats often show an extremely strong attachment to their human owners.

Cats mark their territory in different ways. A cat has special scent glands around its mouth, which it rubs against corners and objects to mark them with its scent. Scratching on objects and urinating in certain places also leave odors that define a cat's invisible borders.

➜ For a happy cat: Allow your cat to retreat into its own space. Cats prefer an elevated perch where they feel safe and can see what is happening around them. This is especially true in homes with more than one cat. Tension between cats is less common when they can stay out of each other's way.

Cats Need Movement

A cat's body is the perfect hunting machine. Its muscles, joints, and body structure are tuned for supple and silent motion, lightning-quick reactions, and excellent coordination—skills that are the envy of even the finest human athletes. Cats by nature lead an active life, honing their abilities in daily practice. A cat that can roam freely outdoors has no difficulty getting the exercise it needs, but indoor cats can

Puff relaxes in a sturdy little hammock.

TIP from the BREEDER

When you choose a cat, don't base your decision solely on its appearance. Find out about the specific characteristics of different breeds. For example, Siamese cats often utter loud, mournful meows, and they thrive on constant activity.

also enjoy vigorous activity. Scratching posts and climbing structures make satisfactory substitutes for the challenges of outdoor terrain. To be sure, most cats have much more fun if they can romp and play with other cats, chasing each other up and down and all around their indoor playground.

Another element of a cat's routine involves patrolling its premises several times a day. Unlike dogs, cats don't have a pack to protect them; therefore, they must inspect their territory themselves to check for intruders or for changes in their surroundings. Making the rounds of the house gives cats a sense of security. This instinctive behavior, together with their need for movement, explains why these freedom-loving felines are happiest when they're moving about.

→ For a happy cat: Don't make life too easy for your kitty. Use your ingenuity to construct a fitness course of obstacles that challenge your cat's physical abilities. You might extend a thick rope across a corner to form a swaying bridge that promotes good balancing skills, or place two elevated platforms up to 5 feet (1.5 meters) apart to encourage cats to practice daring leaps. (See pages 42–46 for more ideas for an indoor playground.)

Grooming

A cat spends a third of the day grooming itself. Caring for its coat like this promotes the cat's well-being. Watching a cat methodically groom its coat can be an almost meditative experience; in fact, the process is just as soothing and calming for the cat itself. A cat that has been frightened or subjected to an unpleasant procedure, such as having its claws trimmed, can relieve its distress by attentively cleaning its fur with its tongue and paws.

Because a cat is so flexible, there is almost no part of its body that it cannot reach with its tongue or teeth. Cats that know and trust each other will also help each other with grooming. This is especially advantageous for those areas that are difficult to reach, like the back of the head. This mutual grooming is also a relic of their kitten days; the cat being groomed is reminded of how sheltered and secure it felt under its mother's protective care.

Stroking your cat's fur gently with your hand arouses similar feelings. To your kitty, your hand feels like a large tongue passing over its coat. Cats that find this tender contact particularly enjoyable may respond by kneading with their paws, or even drooling. These behaviors also stem from their early days, when they suckled at their mother's breast.

➜ For a happy cat: Cats like to be petted, but only when they can relax in peace. Your kitty won't appreciate being forced to cuddle, and it may well express its displeasure with its claws or teeth. A person who is constantly on the move doesn't look like an attractive cuddling partner to a cat. Instead, sit quietly in a comfortable chair and wait for your pet to come to you. Start, as a mother cat does, by stroking the kitty on its head; then let your hand roam slowly down the rest of its body. Be careful, though—many cats are very sensitive on their bellies, and they would rather not be touched there at all.

Cats Are Playful

Most animals play only during their first months of life, under the watchful protection of

their parents. As adults in the wild, they spend much less time in play. Playing can be risky; an animal absorbed in play is less likely to notice what is happening around it and can easily fall victim to a predator.

In the wild, cats scratch at trees to sharpen their claws and mark their territory.

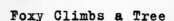

Foxy Climbs a Tree

Moxie had been sitting on the windowsill for quite some time, staring intently at the tall spruce tree outside the window. At first, I thought he must be watching a bird—but when I followed his gaze, there was his friend Foxy, high up in the branches. The cat must have slipped out the kitchen door when I fetched the newspaper. I hastened outside and stood at the base of the tree, craning my neck and calling Foxy's name. Unfortunately, the result was not as I hoped. Instead of responding to my voice, Foxy only climbed higher and higher. What was I to do? I knew better than to climb the tree after him, and I was reluctant to ask the fire department to send a crew with ladders to the rescue. As I stood helpless, a shower of pine needles fell about my head and shoulders. Looking up, I saw Foxy come tumbling down, bouncing head over heels from branch to branch. Without thinking, I held out my arms and caught my little adventurer. As I hugged him to my chest, though, my relief turned to dismay, for Foxy smelled like a spruce-scented bubble bath, and his coat was covered with sticky pine pitch. I brought him inside, tucked him in his plastic carrying box, and called the veterinarian, who advised me to swab the kitty down with warm olive oil. To my surprise, that did remove the pine pitch, but now Foxy looked more like a hedgehog than a cat. His coat was smeared with oil, and the poor little fellow was shivering miserably. One more bath, this time with warm water and cat shampoo, finally restored Foxy to his usual handsome self.

Compared with their wild counterparts, however, domestic cats spend a good deal of time in play. The reason is not that they still need to develop certain skills, but simply that they enjoy being active and are not at risk when they give their full attention to the game. Also, cats who have contact with humans tend to slip back into the role of the kitten relating to its mother cat, so that even older cats still behave in kittenish ways and have fun playing with people.

Unlike other predators, free-roaming cats eagerly pursue small prey at every opportunity, whether they are hungry or not. This insatiable appetite for the hunt has its reasons: In the wild, only about one out of three of a hunting cat's ventures meets with success. If the cat is to survive, it must go after every potential quarry; it can't afford to be lazy.

In domestic cats, this instinctive urge to hunt often finds expression in a tireless enthusiasm for play. This is particularly true of cats who are kept indoors. They don't need to hunt for food, but they savor the joy of the hunt as a playful activity, especially in their younger days. Even a well-fed cat finds any small moving object fascinating. Watch your kitty as it bats a wad of crumpled paper around the room, or pounces on a toy mouse, or pursues a rolling tennis ball— the alert and lively expression on its face clearly says, "I'm doing what I do best, and I'm loving every minute of it!"

Even the rhythm of a cat's day reflects the creature's wild ancestry. Most domestic cats are particularly active in the evening twilight, and this is when they're most likely to demand your attention.

Cats have very expressive body language. Here, the smaller cat clearly wants to be left alone.

Take the time to play with your kitty. Exercise its hunting skills, and give it all the vigorous activity it needs so that it can curl up later on its favorite cushion, relaxed and contented. Be aware that if you don't entertain your cat, it will invent its own entertainment—quite possibly to the detriment of your furniture, your draperies, or your favorite bric-a-brac.

→ For a happy cat: Cats are intelligent creatures; they enjoy mental challenges as well as physical activity. Vary the games you play with your cat, and model them after the natural pastimes of a cat in the wild—chasing a "mouse" across the floor, batting a "bird" out

of the air, or swiping a "fish" from under a blanket.

Cats Can Talk

Ask almost anybody, "What does the kitty say?" The first response that comes to mind is probably "Meow." But meowing is by no means a cat's only way of communicating with other cats, as well as with humans.

Cats can make a wide range of sounds, some of them so distinct that they almost sound like words. Cat owners who know their pets well can tell by the tone of a cat's voice whether it is complaining of hunger, expressing boredom, or

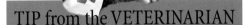

simply saying a friendly good morning. Many breeds tend to be particularly vocal. Siamese cats, for example, are among the most communicative of purebred cats. A Siamese cat may even seem to be telling its owner all the details of a long story.

A cat may utter a cheery murmur with its mouth closed—almost like a chirp—as a way of greeting an approaching cat or its owner. And, of course, everyone is familiar with the purring of a contented cat. Although even experts still don't know for sure how cats make this sound, most people find it very pleasant, and almost nothing is more soothing than to sit quietly with a purring kitty on your lap. Purring can have other meanings as well; kittens purr when they approach older cats to play, and some cats also purr when they are sick or in pain.

Most people know instinctively that it's not a good idea to get any closer to a cat that's hissing. It isn't just the sharp, sibilant sound—also expressively described as "spitting"—that gives the unmistakable warning to stay clear, but also the cat's stiffly arched back and snarling expression. Cats communicate through their body positions and facial expressions in many other situations as well. A typical example is the way a friendly kitty will hold its tail straight up to greet its owner or another familiar person in a gracious sign of welcome.

Cats especially relish fresh running water. They don't like to drink stale water.

TIP from the VETERINARIAN

Cats, especially kittens, are incredibly inquisitive. They will venture anywhere as they explore their world. For your kitty's safety, you should cat-proof your home. (For more information, see Common Hazards, page 38.)

Cats Are Inquisitive

"Curiosity kills the cat" is a familiar saying that experienced cat owners will recognize as not far from the truth. Cats of any age are remarkably inquisitive. Fortunately, their instinctive urge to explore and investigate their surroundings doesn't always have such fatal consequences—and sometimes it even works to their advantage. Stories abound of cats that whisk into the pantry at their owner's heels, or patiently work away until they have figured out how to unlatch a cupboard door. And if a kitty can manage to find and open the jar where the treats are kept, what better reward for an intrepid explorer?

Cats will poke their inquisitive noses into every box, every bucket, every jar—just in case there's something to eat or to play with hidden inside. Such behavior is also a sign of an intelligent mind that thrives on stimulation and challenge. This is a particular concern for cat owners who keep their pet indoors; the cat can easily become bored, because its territory is necessarily limited and may not change much as the seasons pass.

➜ For a happy cat: Foster your cat's intelligence right from the early weeks of its life. Keep offering your pet new and unfamiliar toys; they don't have to be fancy or store-bought. Hide tasty treats in places that challenge a cat's ingenuity as well as its agility. For example, you might tuck a tidbit inside a cardboard tube, then plug each end with a wad of crumpled newspaper (see photo, page 45). Your kitty will have a grand time figuring out how to get at the hidden morsel.

Practice makes perfect—Foxy hones her pouncing skills on a blade of grass.

How Well Do You Know Your Cat?

The first step to taking good care of your cat is learning about its behavior and its needs. Here's a little quiz to see how much you already know about these graceful animals. The answers are given below—but no peeking!

		YES	NO
1	Can cats hear better than humans do?	○	○
2	Do cats leave scent markings when they claw at furniture?	○	○
3	Do cats communicate with body language?	○	○
4	Is a cat's sense of smell keener than a human's?	○	○
5	Should cats drink milk instead of water?	○	○
6	Is it all right to feed a kitty raw pork?	○	○
7	Is the average life span of a cat about 10 years?	○	○
8	Do adult cats lose interest in playing?	○	○
9	Must a kitten learn how to hunt?	○	○
10	Are cats basically solitary creatures?	○	○
11	Does a cat go off by itself to die?	○	○
12	Is purring always an expression of contentedness?	○	○
13	Are cats inquisitive by nature?	○	○

Answers: 1 = yes; 2 = yes; 3 = yes; 4 = yes; 5 = no; 6 = no; 7 = yes; 8 = no; 9 = yes; 10 = no; 11 = yes; 12 = no; 13 = yes.

Building

Moxie is attracted to anything that moves, whether it's a toy or a person's wiggling fingers. Playing gently with a kitten helps it become a good pet— and besides, it's fun for everyone.

Trust
from the Start

love it

TIP from the THERAPIST

Use great caution with kittens and babies. Young cats are curious about everything that moves, and they see a baby's tiny hands and bright eyes as enticing playthings. Their sharp claws can cause serious injury to a small child.

Understanding a Cat's Feelings

Cats are among the most intelligent of domesticated animals. Evidence of this includes their sophisticated body language and their social behavior with other cats and also with humans.

To be sure, cats relate quite differently to other cats and to humans. Other cats are always rivals for food or for a favorite spot. Cats that live together soon develop a social hierarchy that helps to keep the peace among them. Although a cat's relationship with humans might be equally close, it does not share this element of dominance and subordination. Instead, a cat often views its owner as a substitute parent and itself as the baby.

When a cat returns from the hunt and greets its owner with loud meows, it is saying something like "Hi, Mommy, I'm home!" Within seconds, the cat makes the transition from mature hunter to young kitten. Behaviors such as drooling lightly or heavily, or kneading a soft surface with its paws, likewise reflect the mother-child relationship between the human owner and the cat. However, this special relationship stops short of giving the owner control over the cat.

Cats embody a stubborn independence, along with more than a hint of untamable wildness. Perhaps it is just this charming mixture that fascinates cat lovers of all ages.

Your cat may be purring dreamily on your lap while you rub the fur under its chin. In the next moment, spying a bird through the window, it will spring into action, leaping to the windowsill to pursue the feathered creature, if only in its mind.

Contradictions are part of a cat's very nature. On the one hand, cats need peace, quiet, and plenty of sleep; on the other hand, they also need lots of activity and play. This is particularly true of indoor cats, who can't exercise their urge to move and their need to hunt as easily as cats who can roam freely outdoors.

Most of all, kittens less than one year old seek new activity hour by hour; their seemingly unlimited energy can drive their owners to distraction. But don't worry—even though you may sometimes feel that you've brought home a tiger instead of a housecat, sooner or later every kitten will settle down and show its mellow side.

Of course, some cats like to be stroked and petted more than others. However, the experiences of a kitten's first few months are formative in this regard. If a young kitten is constantly picked up, held tight, and cuddled against its will, it will tend to avoid contact with humans. Instead, you should let the kitten take the initiative. Sit quietly on the floor, and when the kitten approaches you, stroke it gently under the chin or behind the ears. Don't grab at your kitty, and let it go when it decides to leave. After a few such pleasurable experiences, the cat will learn to seek you out of its own accord.

Kittens also enjoy romping and playing with their owners. Be careful, though, to keep your hands out of the action. The cat must learn that hands are meant to be used only for petting, not potential victims to be bitten or scratched with their sharp claws.

Your Cat's Wish List

What cats like:

1. Time to play and cuddle with their owner.

2. The company of other cats.

3. Chasing and pouncing on small toys, such as a Ping-Pong ball.

4. A raised platform for sleeping and resting.

5. A scratching post that's also a climbing structure.

6. A cozy seat on the windowsill.

7. Cardboard boxes—just one, or a whole pile—to explore and hide in.

8. Open doors so they can explore rooms at will.

What cats don't like:

1. Frequent or prolonged absences of their owner.

2. Hectic activity, or people who are constantly in motion.

3. Loneliness and boredom.

4. Loud noises.

5. Closed doors that keep them from patrolling their territory every day.

6. Rough play at the hands of a human.

7. A sleeping basket placed at floor level, or a litter box next to their feeding spot.

8. Petting and stroking when they're not in the mood for it.

FREE PUBLIC LIBRARY
KEYPORT NEW JERSEY

When a cat scratches a person, there are two possible reasons: Either the cat has not been taught that scratching is against the rules, or the person has failed to recognize the signals that mean "I've had enough, it's time to take a break." The latter situation often arises with children. It's important to pay attention, keep the child's hands out of the action, and allow the cat to end the game whenever it chooses.

Children and Cats

Children love cats. Cats are fun to play with, their fur is soft and cuddly, and their purring is as fascinating for children as it is for adults. But just as with other pets, children must be taught the right way to treat a cat—not only because the child might hurt the cat, but also because the cat will defend itself if necessary, leaving the marks of its sharp claws or teeth on the child's tender skin. Especially when a new kitten comes into the household, children must learn that although kittens do like to play, they also need time to sleep, time to groom themselves, or even just time to explore their new territory on their own if they are to feel at home.

Moxie and Michael enjoy a relaxing snooze together.

The Stowaway

At last, the suitcases were all packed and piled into the trunk of the car. We were just about to leave on a long-awaited trip to the seashore. Our next-door neighbor had agreed to bring in the mail, water the plants, and take good care of Foxy and Moxie. On the way out the door, I grabbed a wicker basket full of beach towels and set it on the back seat of the car, next to the cooler that held our lunch. Then we were off, elated to be on our way.

Three hours later, we pulled off the highway into a shady rest area to stretch our legs and have a bite to eat. When I turned to fetch the cooler from the back seat, I heard a muffled meow. To my astonishment, the beach towels parted and Moxie's head poked out with a drowsy look of pleasure, as if to say "Here I am, and I'm so glad to see you. Now, what's for lunch?" Obviously, the little fellow had crept into the basket, snuggled down among the towels, and fallen sound asleep.

Faced with another three-hour drive to take Moxie home, we called the friends who had invited us to join them at their beach cottage. To our relief, they generously encouraged us to bring our little stowaway along. After one more phone call to let our neighbor know that Moxie was safe, we continued on our way. As it turned out, Moxie had such a good time at the seashore that we made up our minds to take both kitties with us on our next vacation.

Building Trust Step by Step

The best way to help a new kitten become a trusting and affectionate cat is to proceed slowly.

Start by limiting the kitty's territory to just one room, so it won't be overwhelmed by new impressions. Sit quietly beside the cat's basket and just watch as it explores its new environment. It will no doubt sniff curiously at all the furniture, and a timid kitten might even try to hide under a chair. Be patient; give your new pet plenty of time. Sooner or later, curiosity will overcome timidity, and the cat will emerge from hiding. Most cats will also seek contact with humans. In particular, young kittens who miss their mother soon discover that a person's quiet voice and gentle hands offer the comfort and reassurance they crave. Once your cat has learned to trust you, widen its horizons by taking it on an exploratory tour of the whole house.

Rubbing its head against a person like this is a cat's way of expressing affection and trust.

Cats and Other Pets

"Fighting like cats and dogs" is an expression that need not always apply. Cats and dogs can become good friends if they are allowed to play together from an early age. Given plenty of time, even an older cat can learn to get along with a dog. Of course, there are exceptions; some cats never overcome their natural fear of dogs, and certain breeds of dogs, especially hunting dogs, instinctively see cats as prey and will not leave them in peace. Likewise, cats view small household pets like rats, hamsters, mice, or parakeets as irresistible playthings, at best—and a swipe of the paw can have serious or even fatal consequences for little Tweety or Squeaky.

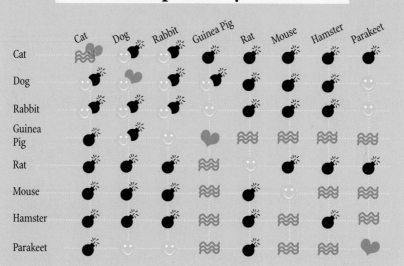

Compatibility Test

	Cat	Dog	Rabbit	Guinea Pig	Rat	Mouse	Hamster	Parakeet
Cat	Indifferent	Fur will fly	Fur will fly	Fur will fly	Fur will fly	Fur will fly	Fur will fly	Fur will fly
Dog	Fur will fly	Get along best	Fur will fly	Fur will fly	Fur will fly	Fur will fly	Fur will fly	Can learn to get along
Rabbit	Fur will fly	Fur will fly	Fur will fly	Can learn to get along	Fur will fly	Fur will fly	Fur will fly	Can learn to get along
Guinea Pig	Fur will fly	Fur will fly	Can learn to get along	Get along best	Indifferent	Indifferent	Indifferent	Indifferent
Rat	Fur will fly	Fur will fly	Fur will fly	Indifferent	Fur will fly	Can learn to get along	Fur will fly	Fur will fly
Mouse	Fur will fly	Fur will fly	Fur will fly	Indifferent	Fur will fly	Can learn to get along	Indifferent	Indifferent
Hamster	Fur will fly	Fur will fly	Fur will fly	Indifferent	Fur will fly	Indifferent	Fur will fly	Indifferent
Parakeet	Fur will fly	Can learn to get along	Can learn to get along	Indifferent	Fur will fly	Indifferent	Indifferent	Get along best

 Get along best   *Fur will fly*   ≋ *Indifferent to each other*   *Can learn to get along*

4 Play Together

Playing with your cat is fun, of course, but it's also a good way to make friends. The cat learns that it has nothing to fear even if you should make a sudden motion. After a time, your pet comes to associate you with everything positive: food, companionship, petting, and play. Use your imagination to help your kitten develop its physical skills while you have a good time together.

5 Fast Friends

Before long, your new friend will trust you completely. More and more often, the kitty will take the initiative to interact with you. It will rub itself along your legs, jump into your lap, and press its little head against your chin. Now and then, your cat will even extend a clear and irresistible invitation to play.

6 Completely Relaxed

You'll know when your cat really trusts you—it will cuddle close, lie down on its side, and practically demand to be stroked. At this point, you might cautiously attempt to pet the cat's more sensitive areas, such as its paws and belly. From now on, you can anticipate many soothing hours of relaxed companionship.

1 Arouse Its Curiosity

Make yourself comfortable, because your cat will set the pace as you get acquainted. You can attract its attention by talking quietly or making the little kissing sounds that cats find so inviting. When your kitty approaches you, take care to avoid any sudden movements. Keep your voice low, because loud noises will startle the cat and make it wary.

2 Offer a Treat

There's nothing wrong with a little bribery to help your kitty lose its shyness and associate you with positive experiences. At first, offer your cat only a portion of its food in its food dish; feed it the rest by hand, bit by bit. Of course, you can't apply this technique until your cat will approach to be fed, but after that your pet will quickly learn that good things come from your hand.

3 Petting and Stroking

When your cat seems comfortable in your presence, slowly try to stroke its fur. Talk in a soothing voice as you cautiously rub your fingers under its chin or behind its ears. Don't try to hold it firmly. The cat should always have the feeling that it is free to leave. Stroke the kitty on its head at first, and then down its back.

Indoor Adventures

After a catnap on a cozy cushion, then a thorough grooming, it's time for kitty to explore the house. Though every nook and cranny is familiar territory, there's always something new to discover. Especially in their early years, cats will happily turn the household into their own adventure playground. Even the inexperienced cat owner soon learns the importance of cat-proofing every room in the house. If you don't clear the breakfast dishes at once, expect to see the traces of a cat's rough tongue on the butter dish; if you leave the milk and cookies unattended, don't be surprised to find a kitty lapping eagerly from a milky puddle.

Small items of jewelry are also favorite playthings; they smell like their owner, they glitter enticingly in the sunlight, and a kitty can bat them around on the floor—until they disappear under the dresser or the refrigerator.

Best of all, however, cats like to play with another cat or a familiar person.

Bebop never tires of playing peek-a-boo.

Pretty Please, with Cream on Top

My daughter Vanessa and my cat Foxy have
the same birthday. For her sixth birthday
party, Vanessa asked for chocolate cake,
topped with her favorite strawberries and
whipped cream. This year, she also made a
special treat for the kitties. Chopping up a hard-
boiled egg, she mixed it with a bit of crabmeat,
some cottage cheese, and a spoonful of canned cat
food, then formed the mixture into a little cake
and topped it with a sprig of parsley.

Later that afternoon, as the doorbell rang, I
set the two birthday cakes side by side on the
kitchen counter and went to help my daughter greet
her guests. Vanessa could hardly wait to tell the
other children about the treat that was in store.
Proudly, she led them to the kitchen and opened
the door. From the hallway, I heard them burst
into gales of laughter—and indeed, it was a comi-
cal sight. Moxie and Foxy crouched beside the
chocolate cake, covered from ear to ear with
whipped cream and reaching for more. Meanwhile,
their own little cake stood untouched.

Quick as a wink, Vanessa scooped the uninvited
guests onto the floor, where they
began to clean their faces
and paws. While she opened
her presents, I baked a
batch of chocolate cup-
cakes, replenished the
strawberries, and whipped
another pint of cream.
As Vanessa blew out
the candles on her
cupcake, the children
agreed that this had
been a birthday party
to remember.

Fun and Games

Cats of all ages love to play. This feather duster is
Moxie's favorite toy. When Kathleen waves it back and
forth above his head, he swipes at it as if it were
a little bird. Now and then, the mighty hunter even
catches a feather or two.

with Cats

have fun

An Adventure Playground for Cats

All cats need plenty of activity and stimulation for their physical and mental well-being. Such exercise is especially important for cats who spend most or all of their time indoors. Many cats will even learn to do tricks. Shadow, for example, will jump from one chair to another on command. Here's how Shadow learned the trick: We put two chairs side by side, with the cat on one chair and a favorite treat on the other. When we said "Jump!," Shadow made the leap. Little by little, we moved the chairs apart, and Shadow leapt farther each time, like a feline circus star. (Of course, this won't work unless your kitty is in the mood for gymnastic stunts, and you must stop the lesson when the cat loses interest.)

Jump, Shadow, jump! It's amazing how far and how high these agile creatures can leap.

What Kind of Play Does Your Cat Prefer?

Cats play in many different ways. Some games involve objects; others are more about movement. Two cats may play together as partners, or they may engage in friendly tussles. Observe your own cats as they play. What games do they prefer?

	YES	NO
1 Does your kitten often leap into the air?	○	○
2 Does your cat run pell-mell around the house?	○	○
3 Do your cats scuffle playfully with each other?	○	○
4 Does your kitty like to laze around with other cats or with you?	○	○
5 Does your cat climb whenever it has the chance?	○	○
6 Does your cat enjoy stalking another cat?	○	○
7 Does your kitty have fun batting a soft toy or crumpled paper around on the floor?	○	○
8 Does your cat like to hide?	○	○
9 Does your cat like to pounce on a moving object, as if catching a mouse?	○	○
10 Will your kitty pursue anything that makes a rustling sound?	○	○

Key: If you checked Yes to questions 7, 9, and 10, your cat likes to play with objects; Yes to 1, 2, and 5, enjoys movement play; Yes to 3 and 6, enjoys friendly competition; Yes to 4 and 8, likes partner play.

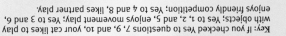

Cats Need Playtime

At first it might seem that playing is an unnecessary luxury for animals—a waste of time and energy. However, a cat's natural inclination to play serves a useful purpose, developing skills the animal will need in later life. As kittens play, they improve their agility and strength. They also learn to understand the body movement and communication signals of other cats and animals.

Three-week-old kittens already engage in rough-and-tumble play with their littermates. As the weeks go by, these games become more complicated and begin to incorporate elements from another sphere: the hunt. Kittens instinctively practice the techniques for stalking a mouse, pouncing on a bird, or catching a fish—all essential skills for a cat's survival in the wild.

Each of these hunting skills involves a sequence of individual movements. For example, stalking a mouse or other small animal requires hiding, watching, lying in wait, creeping up and pouncing on the prey, holding it tight, and finally killing it. To catch a bird, the cat must often leap high into the air and swipe at the bird in mid-flight to knock it to the ground. Cats hone their fishing skills, even without water, by seizing an object on the floor, tossing it behind them, then turning in a flash to grab it again and carry it away.

Foxy must have heard the can opener in the kitchen! Even the most skilled athletes marvel at the agility of a cat.

How Happy Is Your Cat?

How much do you hear your cat purring each day?	◯ Not at all *0 points*	◯ 20 minutes *1 point*	◯ More *2 points*
How much time does your cat spend moving around the house or outdoors?	◯ None *0 points*	◯ 1 hour *1 point*	◯ More *3 points*
Does your kitty take advantage of opportunities for exercise?	◯ Yes *2 points*	◯ No *0 points*	
What does your cat's coat look like?	◯ Glossy *2 points*	◯ Dull *0 points*	
Do your cats fight with each other every day?	◯ No *3 points*	◯ Yes *0 points*	
How does your cat react when you approach it?	◯ Runs away *0 points*	◯ Pulls back *1 point*	◯ Stays put *3 points*
How often does your cat groom itself each day?	◯ Often *3 points*	◯ Sometimes *1 point*	◯ Never *0 points*
Does your kitty seek contact with you?	◯ Never *0 points*	◯ Rarely *1 point*	◯ Often *3 points*
Does your cat respond when you invite it to play?	◯ Readily *3 points*	◯ Sometimes *1 point*	◯ Never *0 points*
Does your kitty lie on its side in a relaxed posture to sleep?	◯ Never *0 points*	◯ Rarely *1 point*	◯ Often *3 points*
Does your cat purr with pleasure when you pet it?	◯ Never *0 points*	◯ Rarely *1 point*	◯ Often *3 points*

0–10 points: This cat has problems. **10–18 points:** Could be better. **18–25 points:** Good, but not great. **25–30 points:** The cat is as happy as can be.

Early Morning Gift

Foxy and Moxie, like all cats, are hunters by nature. Every now and then they bring us a small dead offering to admire, usually a mouse they cornered in the basement. The other morning, my husband and I were still sound asleep in bed. As the sun streamed in the open window, I began to wake up, slowly becoming aware of the weight of two cats on the blankets. I wasn't surprised, because Foxy and Moxie often come to snuggle with us in the morning. Drowsily, I opened my eyes. Suddenly, I was jolted wide awake. Right in front of my face, a tiny gray mouse dangled from Moxie's jaws, struggling for its very life. When I shrieked in horror, my husband bolted out of bed, and Moxie dropped the mouse. In a flash, the terrified creature scampered across the blankets, skittered up the curtain that hung at the window, and barricaded itself behind the curtain rod. Foxy and Moxie immediately took off in hot pursuit, leaping to the curtains and clawing their way to the top. But the mouse—both nimble and clever—managed to evade its pursuers. When Moxie and Foxy realized that their prey had escaped, they made their way back down the curtains, clearly disappointed. However, they soon got over it, for they knew the bed was warm and cozy. Before long, the four of us had settled down among the blankets to start the day over in peace.

Adult cats still exercise their hunting skills, whether they need to eat the prey or are fed as pets. In a cat's hunting games, any small movable object can serve as target and victim. A small ball of yarn, Granny's heirloom ruby earring, a dangerously sharp knitting needle— all look like fair game to a kitty on the prowl. Some cats will even invent their own pastimes, like sliding down the back of the sofa or tossing a neat stack of newspapers to the four corners of the room. The prudent cat owner will take measures to protect both the kitty and the furniture.

As a cat grows older, it spends less time in active play. But even an elderly cat will usually respond to an invitation to join its favorite game. A cat that won't play at all is probably tired, sick, or very old indeed. For the most part, cats just plain love to play.

TIP from the PET STORE

The ideal toy for a cat is very lightweight, can be batted a long way with a swipe of the paw, and maybe even makes noise when it moves. Cats love all kinds of little balls, toys with bells, bundles of colorful feathers, and fuzzy toy mice.

Cats are intrigued by anything that rustles. What's more, a pile of dry leaves may hide an interesting surprise.

Active and Happy

Dover is getting on in years, but he's still an active kitty. To be sure, he doesn't pounce as accurately as before on a ball that's in motion, or leap as nimbly onto the counter for a drink of running water, but he usually succeeds on the second try. Best of all, however, he likes to curl up in his favorite armchair beside his favorite person for a nice round of petting.

in Old Age

old & happy

How Long Do Cats Live?

The average life expectancy for cats is about 12 years, though it varies according to their living conditions. Given proper care, a domestic cat can live much longer than its wild counterparts. Cats ordinarily live for 9 to 15 years, and they usually do not begin to decline until their final year. If you observe your cat as time goes by, you will no doubt notice the changes in appearance and behavior that let you know your feline friend is growing old.

The Older Cat

The most obvious sign of old age is stiffness in the joints, which causes the cat to move more slowly and with less enjoyment. It cannot jump as far or as high as before.

In fact, an older cat might miss its target when it leaps, possibly even tumbling to the floor. However, chances are it probably won't hurt itself when this happens. Although not as agile as it once was, an older cat almost always lands on its feet.

The Autumn of Life

→ **Behavior:**
With age, cats become more mellow. They're not as interested in everything new; in fact, they'd rather not have changes in their daily routine.

→ **Coat:**
The cat's fur begins to look somewhat dull.

→ **Motion:**
An older cat's joints are stiffer and its movements slower. It likes to rest in a sunny spot, and it spends more time sleeping.

→ **Vision and Hearing:**
A cat's vision and hearing usually decline as it grows old.

→ **Diet:**
Age has little effect on a cat's appetite. In some cases, however, cats may become more finicky eaters in their old age.

→ **Hygiene:**
Older cats continue to groom themselves but typically not as well as they once did. If a cat's joints are stiff, it might not be able to bend far enough to reach its back or other areas with its tongue. You might have to help it stay clean.

→ **Health:**
An older cat is more vulnerable to illness because its immune system is weaker. Bladder infections are more common.

Increasing stiffness in the cervical spine may make it more difficult for the cat to groom certain areas, such as the lower back or the base of the tail. If your older kitty's coat begins to look matted and unkempt, you should gently brush or comb your pet more often to help it stay clean.

On the whole, an aging cat becomes more mellow; it spends more time sleeping, cat-napping, or just quietly watching the world go by. Its favorite spot will be warm and sunny, comfortably padded, and elevated to offer protection and a good view of the family's activities. The outdoor environment is increasingly dangerous for an older cat. It will be at a disadvantage in altercations with a younger rival, and because its vision and hearing are less acute, an older cat is more vulnerable to automobiles and similar hazards. Elderly cats are well aware of their own deficiencies, and they will usually adopt a more sedate lifestyle, enjoying the comfortable dignity of a senior citizen.

An older cat is more vulnerable to illness, because its immune system is not as strong as before. Quite often, the gums and the roots of the teeth become inflamed. When chewing hard foods becomes painful, the cat will refuse to eat its dry food; this is an early sign of inflammation inside the mouth.

"Aah, that feels good." What could be more relaxing than a snooze in the sunshine?

TIP from the VETERINARIAN

Each of a cat's eyes has a third eyelid, called the *nictitating membrane*, that protects and lubricates the eyes. If this eyelid remains prolapsed, it may be a sign of weakness or serious illness. Take the cat to the veterinarian without delay.

Bladder infections, another common age-related problem, make it painful for the cat to urinate and should be suspected if an older cat begins to leave unexpected puddles around the house. Puddles could indicate other health problems as well. So it's a good idea to schedule your older cat's regular visits to the veterinarian at more frequent intervals, because the early diagnosis and treatment of any illness can help to spare your pet unnecessary suffering. It's also advisable to adjust a cat's diet as it grows old. Pet stores sell special food for older cats. Vitamin and mineral supplements and digestive aids can help to prevent nutritional deficiencies or constipation.

Although a cat's senses definitely decline in its old age, the animal somehow manages to compensate for this decline far longer than humans do.

Young cats thrive on new experiences, but older cats are often much less interested in novelty. Instead, they tend to be upset if their daily routine is disturbed, for example, by unfamiliar visitors or a new baby in the household.

Moving to a new home can be very stressful for an old cat. Furthermore, although a cat owner who brings home a lively kitten to provide amusement for an older cat may mean well, most old cats would much prefer to be left in peace and quiet.

How Cats Die

A cat will often go off by itself to die. This happens especially if the cat is in pain. The cat doesn't understand what causes the pain, so it tries to escape by hiding in a dark corner.

A cat's death is much like that of other animals. As death approaches, the cat eats little or nothing, moves about less and less, and finally just stays curled up in its sleeping spot. Animals who die of old age usually do not appear to suffer. Many a pet, apparently sensing that the end is near, choose to spend their final hours with their owners. Lying peacefully beside this lifelong friend, the old cat quietly breathes its last, like a candle burning out.

The situation is different if a cat has an incurable and painful illness. In that case, it is the owner's responsibility to consult a veterinarian about measures that will spare the cat great pain or prolonged suffering.

Saying Good-bye

Most people are very fond of their cats and feel grief when a cat dies. The loss of this household companion brings a sad change to the daily routine. All at once, everything is different—no more early morning greeting, no demanding meows for food, no insistent rubbing against the ankles, no amusing antics, no purring presence to warm the lap at night. These natural feelings of loss and pain should be taken seriously, and even outsiders should do what they can to help.

Younger family members will experience a similar flood of emotions when a beloved cat dies. They too have woven the pet into their lives. So it is only natural that they will miss their kitty intensely.

Furthermore, this may be a child's first encounter with the finality of death. One way to console a grieving child is to explain that animals are not afraid of dying. They simply experience death, like birth, as a natural part of life.

After many long years of companionship, these two old friends understand each other very well.

For many children, the initial shock of grief soon gives way to concern about their pet's final journey. Their faithful friend deserves respect, even after death. Helping to bury the cat's body in a peaceful resting place can make it easier for a child to express sad feelings, but also to talk about happy memories of the kitty who has died.

When One Cat Dies

When several cats live in the same household, the death of one cat can affect the others. Often-times, one cat will obviously miss a companion that has died. If the surviving cat appears to be lonely, Bach flower essences may bring relief. These herbal remedies may also help people who are grieving for a departed cat. Giving a forlorn kitty extra attention and affection will probably console both the cat and the owner. In some cases—provided that the remaining cat is not already too old to get used to a completely new partner—it can be a good idea to bring home another cat.

Use caution and common sense when introducing a new cat. It's advisable to start the newcomer out in a cage where the old-timer can see it and smell it, but not reach it. This allows the two cats to get acquainted with each other safely, without the risk of a traumatic first encounter. After a while, you can open the door of the cage and let the new cat explore the household and get to know its residents at its own pace.

Almost every older cat will appreciate the gentle warmth of a soothing massage.

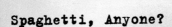

Spaghetti, Anyone?

Moxie and Foxy know very well that the dinner table is off-limits for them. But every now and then, a particularly savory aroma tempts them into forgetting their good manners. Last night, as we were enjoying spaghetti with a delicious cream sauce, Moxie and Foxy couldn't resist. One from the left, one from the right, they hopped up onto the table. Firmly, we plopped them back down onto the floor, but instead of banishing them from the room, I held out a strand of spaghetti.

Bold little Moxie ate it as if he'd been dining on pasta all his life. Next, it was Foxy's turn. He pawed at the dangling oddity, tentatively at first, then with more vigor. Before he had quite figured out what to do, one end of the strand of spaghetti had stuck to his shoulder. Twisting and turning every which way, Foxy tried to dislodge it, but to no avail—his frantic contortions only caused the spaghetti to flap wildly about. Soon, even Moxie was alarmed. He leaped to the top of the sideboard, where he could observe the fray from a safe distance, while the rest of us looked on in helpless laughter.

At long last, the spaghetti fell from Foxy's shoulder to the floor. Cautiously, he backed away, still panting from his exertions. Chuckling, I offered him another strand, but he would have none of it. Instead, he retreated to the living room and spent the rest of the dinner hour grooming his coat and restoring his customary calm.

Index

Dr. Astrid Schubert
is a veterinarian specializing in behavioral therapy for dogs, cats, and horses. In the course of her study of modern methods of behavioral therapy, she has traveled to England and the United States. She presents seminars on the behavior and training of household pets, and her articles appear regularly in specialized journals.

Monika Wegler
is one of the leading animal photographers in Europe. The author of several books about animals, she also breeds Abyssinian cats. The photographs in this book feature her own seven cats.

Gabriele Linke-Grün
works as a freelance writer for the Gräfe und Unzer nature book series and for various animal magazines and textbook publishers. She wrote the *Cat Adventures*.

With wide-eyed curiosity, kittens observe the world around them.

Books

Behrend, Katrin. *Cats*. Hauppauge, NY: Barron's Educational Series, Inc., 1999.

Davis, Karen Leigh. *Compatible Cats*. Hauppauge, NY: Barron's Educational Series, Inc., 2001.

Davis, Karen Leigh. *The Cat Handbook*. Hauppauge, NY: Barron's Educational Series, Inc., 2000.

Rittrich-Dorenkamp. *Playing with Cats*. Hauppauge, NY: Barron's Educational Series, Inc., 2000.

Magazines

Cat Fancy
P.O. Box 52864
Boulder, CO 80322-2864
(800) 365-4421

Cat Fancier's Almanac
1805 Atlantic Avenue
P.O. Box 1005
Manasquan, NJ 08736-0805
(732) 528-9797

Cats
P.O. Box 420240
Palm Coast, FL 32142-0014
(904) 445-2818

I Love Cats
950 Third Avenue, 16th Floor
New York, NY 10022-2705
(212) 888-1855

Organizations

American Association of Cat Enthusiasts (AACE)
P.O. Box 213
Pine Brook, NJ 07058
(973) 335-6717
Web page:
http://www.aaceinc.org

American Cat Association (ACA)
8101 Katherine Avenue
Panorama City, CA 91402
(818) 781-5656

Acknowledgments

The photographer and the publisher wish to thank Bärbel and Max Ehrl, who built the scratching board, scratching posts, and climbing rope shown on pages 6–7 and 43–44. At their cat specialty store in Munich, they provide advice for cat owners as well as cat safety netting for balconies and yards.

English translation
© Copyright 2002 by
Barron's Educational Series, Inc.

Original title of the book
in German is
Meine Katze und ích

Copyright © 2000 by Gräfe und
Unzer Verlag GmbH, Munich

English translation by
Celia Bohannon

All rights reserved.

No part of this book may be reproduced in any form, by photostat, microfilm, xerography, or any other means, or incorporated into any information retrieval system, electronic or mechanical, without the written permission of the copyright owner.

*All inquiries should
be addressed to:*
Barron's Educational Series, Inc.
250 Wireless Boulevard
Hauppauge, NY 11788
http://www.barronseduc.com

*International Standard Book
No. 0-7641-1924-9*

Library of Congress Catalog Card
No. 00-112038

Printed in Hong Kong

9 8 7 6 5 4 3 2